Finding the Normal
in the
Abnormal

Four-Week Bible Study Book

Haley Kelley

ISBN 979-8-88616-815-0 (paperback)
ISBN 979-8-88616-816-7 (digital)

Christian Faith Publishing
832 Park Avenue
Meadville, PA 16335
www.christianfaithpublishing.com

Printed in the United States of America

Before we begin this one-month study broken down into four weeks, there are a few things I want you to think about. I want you to go into this Bible study expecting to release things you cannot hold onto, things you were not destined to battle by yourself. We serve a mighty God; we serve a sovereign God. Despite the hardships we endure in this broken world, He is everything He says He is and will be for us in our lives. I want you to bring every piece of yourself into this four-week Bible study, and I want you to be honest with yourself, with your season of life, with your vision of what life should look like. And because our God is in fact a savior, He has provided ways to heal and deliver us.

He's given us a book of promises (the Bible) to preserve us all by His grace and His love. Our salvation cannot be stolen based on our bad days, shortcomings, and mistakes. We live in a broken world, and because of that, we must focus our eyes on eternity and not the temporary. When I began this Bible study writing process, the Holy Spirit gave me two sentences that I felt you needed to hear before starting this: *God loves you. He hears you. He sees your tears. He's not left you. He's not nor will He ever forsake you. It's time to walk out a life full of surrender and in submission to Him and His will for your life.*

Our vision of life can really be misaligned and blurred when everything about it looks abnormal. It looks abnormal because we've based our lives and what they should look like off the world's vision and expectations rather than God's vision and expectations.

> Do not love this world nor the things it offers you,
> for when you love the world, you do not have the
> love of the Father in you. For the world offers

only a craving for physical pleasure, a craving for everything we see, and pride in our achievements and possessions; these are not from the Father but are from this world. And this world is fading away, along with everything that people crave. But anyone who does what pleases God will live forever. (1 John 2:15–17 NLT)

Don't copy the behavior and customs of this world, but let God transform you into a new person by changing the way you think. Then you will learn to know God's will for you, which is good and pleasing and perfect. (Romans 12:2 NLT)

We feel like we've lost control and, essentially, we become anxious, depressed, and even angry sometimes. We become depleted, chasing down answers when the answers are as simple as just surrendering to His will. Whenever we can realign our values to match God's values, our integrity can remain intact despite the difficult seasons and the hardships we face. It can remain intact because we know we serve a God that can, in fact, use our disappointments, sins, and heartaches to minster to other broken people. And when this happens, we find hope. A hope where we come to the table expecting fulfillment of the promises God's made to us. The outcome will always be favorable to us because He favors us. He is smitten with us. He is absolutely smitten with you.

F—aith
A—cquires
I—ntegirty
T—hrough
H—ope

But please remember, despite your shortcomings (because you are not perfect), He still loves and values you. Your faith may waver in your walk, but God's love does not. It's not a conditional love, but it is every bit of unconditional. God knew you would mess up; He knew you would fall short, and He still sent His son to die on the cross to bear the sins of yours and mine. That's love that's every bit as reckless. That's a love I never knew until I knew God, fully knew Him.

And in knowing Him, I had to surrender. I had to receive.

I hope in this study you will receive His love for you.

Grab a pencil, get cozy, maybe get a cup of coffee, and let's start our first piece for the month together!

Week 1

I was sitting in an old beater car in the crowded streets of Haiti, looking over all the rummage that was piled higher than most of the buildings back home. Livestock just running free everywhere, and girls at a shockingly young age standing outside in clothing I was unsure I could find remotely appropriate. My mind was racing, *Why are they wearing that?*

I had agreed to come here on a mission trip at the last minute. Specifically speaking, I said, "Yes, if God wants me to go, He will make it happen."

Clearly, He wanted me here, and He made it happen. The moment leading up to this was something comical—you could probably find yourself watching it on a reality TV show while shoveling a handful of popcorn into your mouth. I had to raise enough funds in nine days to be able to go—nine days—impossible! I was living paycheck to paycheck as a single mom, and I had no extra funds to cough up for a trip across the world, much less to cover groceries and rent for the week. I prayed for God's will in it, and seven days later, I had exceeded the funds that were needed.

Let's take a moment to reflect on the next hurdle, a passport. I had never flown out of the country before and, clearly, never had a need for a passport. I put a rush order in as I was going to need it to arrive sooner rather than later. With the rush, it was expected to arrive seven days before we flew out. Except, it never arrived. After attempting to track it down and many phone calls later, it was clear that my passport somehow got lost! At that point, I called the head office located in Chicago (where they print the passports), and I explained the significance of this trip. Some sweet, soft-spoken angel on the other end of the phone agreed to redo it and ship it again at their expense. Except, once again, it never arrived. (Guys, I can't make this stuff up!) I was flying out the next night, and I had no passport, and I was convinced that this was it. This was God's way of saying, *Not now.*

I sat with my godmother, expressing the moment of sheer defeat, and she reminded me that this could very well be the enemy's way of trying to stop me, and there was an alternative. How committed was I to what God had called me to do? So my godfather and I loaded up in the car, and we drove all the way to the Chicago office to arrive there by morning for whenever they opened their doors. We drove over six hours, and we arrived to find out they wouldn't be able to have it printed until after lunch, so we waited, we ate, and we drank a lot more coffee. We were running on no sleep, and the exhaustion was setting in. Caffeine didn't seem to put a dent in the exhaustion, but I kept throwing them back. We finally received the passport, and we headed home in a rush as I now needed to get to the airport; I literally walked through the door, got my luggage, and turned around and left to meet everyone at the church to leave for our flight.

Leading up to this very moment, I had spent the last year of my life experiencing the "fire" you hear so many Christians talk about, and my heart wanted Jesus more than it ever had. I longed for Him in a way I never knew or could fathom. But here I was in a foreign country that had poverty-ridden streets and towns—with people I didn't even know. I was questioning at that very moment why exactly He had brought me here. I look back in my journal to reflect on the memories to find a note that says, "*My heart broke for the broken that day.*"

Nothing about where I was seemed normal, and my heart was not exactly prepared for it. As we journeyed further down the streets of Yvon, Haiti, there was something that caught my eye on the busy side street. Something that rocked my world in a way I could never forget. And once my eyes fixated on it, I couldn't break them free. There was a man sitting in a chair, a broken lawn chair, and our eyes locked. The car sat in its place for what felt like a decade in bumper-to-bumper traffic as we just stared at each other. The problem was, I couldn't see anything past his eyes. It was an emptiness I had never

ever seen so loudly before in my life. One that I would forever carry with me. Tears began to stream slowly down my face, and I quickly wiped them away before the strangers I was with saw them.

We had a long trip into the village that night, and my heart could not shake what I was experiencing or feeling. I had had no more than a catnap over the last three days; clearly, I was exhausted, but I had to write it down. My journal reflection was, "I am a little angry at God. I don't get it. Why? Why did I have to come here? Wasn't this trip supposed to be about growth and helping other people? To talk to people about Jesus. Why?"

Reading that now, I know there was a strange anger behind my why.

I don't think I was fully prepared for the work Jesus was ready to do in me that week: the breakthroughs, the self-evaluation, the self-reflection. I tell people Jesus helped me take inventory that week. But essentially, he showed me how the heart He created in me was much like His. How it, too, broke for the broken. How He longs for them, for me, for you—the broken.

> The sacrifice you desire is a broken spirit. You
> will not reject a broken and repentant heart. O
> God. (Psalm 51:17 NLT)

It was throughout that week that I realized that God had brought me through the brokenness the world had intended to destroy me with so He could help break me back down again. But in a way that He Himself had intended for me. I want you to envision peeling an onion—it was kind of like that—a nasty onion (sorry, onion lovers), peeling back a layer at a time, and if you're like me, crying relentlessly while doing so. Some of the peeling was kind of painful and a lot of raw (no pun intended). But in such a way where the walls I had spent most of my adult life building and defending, would begin to crumble at His soft whisper, and I could then begin to grow into the woman He wanted me to be. There was no coincidence in the man I had seen on the busy side street becoming my focal point that day. Maybe it was because the emptiness and brokenness that I saw through his eyes, that darkness that I felt radiating from him, used to be me. And maybe, just maybe, some days—it still was.

Darkness, defined in spiritual terms, is that of one who is closed off, blinded or evil; it's considered a place of punishment. I was blinded, closed off, and guarded.

My heart wanted more, but as far as how to get it, I was clueless. I felt as if I was wearing a mask, even though my life had taken a complete turn over the last year.

It was that week, as I was talking to the children about the wonderful Jesus we served, that everything really became full circle for me. I was talking to the kids that day about faith. I obviously had a translator as I could not speak Creole, and I remember asking a question that brought a whole new level of heaviness. I asked the children if they'd ever prayed for something and never seen it "come to life." If maybe they'd prayed for something, but it hadn't exactly been answered yet. I remember this young boy, with a radiant smile, excitedly speaking to my translator in response to my question as I stood by anxiously waiting for the translation.

My translator looked over to me and said so nonchalantly, "He said that he prayed for shoes for a long time and did not receive shoes, but he is so happy because he gets to wake up every day and your team brought them food!"

I choked back the tears, smiled, and nodded my head. A small jolt of anger began to fizzle up within, and I quickly shoved it back down. I could not make sense of his excitement about this in that moment. I couldn't understand how so simple of a prayer couldn't have been answered for him. This young boy only asked for shoes. That, to me, was a simple prayer. To me, that prayer should have been answered. To me, I was angry that a God with so much love for His children didn't answer this "small" prayer. Oh, but that's the thing. The power behind his answer moved mountains in my heart. The power behind this little boy's waiting season started a movement in me.

It was weeks later, after returning home, when I realized the significance in my life that the man on the busy side street carried, the power of the little boy's unanswered prayer. It was when I realized that I had everything here, stateside, and took it all for granted, and yet they had nothing and had a more thankful heart than I ever had or could probably ever have. This little boy wasn't mad at his unanswered prayer because his focus wasn't on what he didn't get. His focus was on Jesus Himself. His focus was on what he did have in that moment rather than what he hadn't yet received. The man on the side street broke my heart because I was once, too, the empty broken vessel of a human. I had a heart problem, and it took me going across the country to even realize it. The world had me captive in believing that the things I struggled with were normal because everyone struggles. But when we have Jesus, we have hope that our struggles and pain do not cease without purpose.

There's going to be a time when you're walking through the darkness and the only thing you have is the Word. The only thing you have are the promises of the Lord. And whether your prayers are answered or they aren't answered, you forever have the ability to tap into the power of the Holy Spirit to help carry you through times the enemy intended for you to very much be destroyed by. This little boy—he could have very much been defeated in agony of pain from his feet constantly beating against the ground and rocks cutting through them. However, his focus wasn't on the pain. It was on the promises; it was on the promise maker. His pain had a purpose, and whether he knew it then or not, that purpose in that moment was to help me realize how valuable a relationship with Christ is despite what He gives or doesn't give us. That despite our feelings in the seasons of unknown, He is still sovereign.

Note: Pain is only without purpose when we do not allow it to help shape and mold us to help others.

The enemy seems to get a front-row invite whenever we are standing in the darkness. One letting him know to come join us, tempt us, discourage us, lie to us. He knows he can join us where we stand in the darkness, and then he delivers to you every lie possible to keep your focus on the darkness rather than the target or goal itself. The enemy knows when you are in an insanely vulnerable place. He knows the only thing you are seeing and will see is the darkness if he can just step in and throw your focus off.

Example: Whenever you go and shoot a bow and arrow, do you focus on the bull's-eye? Or do you focus on everything surrounding the bull's-eye? Your focus should be on the bull's-eye, obviously. If you shift your view from the bull's-eye to the surrounding area, that's where your arrow will follow because that's where your eyes are looking.

It's very much a resemblance of our hearts and our minds. Where our minds wander, our hearts will follow. And if my focus is on the darkness, the enemy's lies begin to look a lot like promises, and the light of Jesus is no longer the focal point. It's no longer the bull's-eye. Things can become very tricky when we cannot discern between that of the enemy and that of Christ.

I had spent much of my life running and hiding from the things that broke me, the places I got stuck, and the people who had hurt me. It was right then, in that very moment, that God was bringing me to a place to confront the things that had held me captive. My season of growth had to start with a season of truth. Once I became willing, it became clear that I had to shift my magnifying glass to the root of my problems, and that was my heart. I could not bear good fruit holding on to all the bad fruit; there simply wasn't enough room.

Everything we do in this life will flow from within; it will flow from our hearts. The Word tells us repeatedly to guard our hearts (see below the Bible study scriptures for references). When we allow the bad things that we've experienced to take root, we allow those things to drown out the good things. It's just like tending to a garden bed; if I go and plant tomatoes, potatoes, peppers, and onions (bulbs) in the garden and I never go back to the garden to tend to the weeds, the plants will be swallowed up by the weeds (which do not produce fruit). We allow the enemy a front-row seat in our garden to use the baggage that has taken root not only in our hearts but now in our lives. He knows our struggles, and his very intention is to take those to use against us. His mission is to completely stop, paralyze, and hinder us in our callings, our relationships, and our careers.

Bible passages to read:

- Ephesians 4:17–31
- Luke 6:45
- Matthew 12:33–37
- Galatians 5:22–23

Notes:

Whenever we harden our hearts, we put up walls that keep people out, including Jesus. We unintentionally (and sometimes intentionally) pull away from the peacemaker in the process of life. Typically, this is some type of trauma response. Whenever we separate our lives from Christ because of the hardening of our hearts, we become less intentional in our efforts to work at an everyday relationship with Jesus. We, in most cases, blame the wrong person for our heart problems. Which ultimately leads us to become insensitive regarding sin and our own selfish desires and motives.

Self-evaluation time

1. Do you feel as if you're walking through life behind a mask? If so, what's brought you to the point of putting one on? Was it abuse, maybe rejection, or maybe abandonment? Write it down. Be honest with yourself.

_____

_____

_____

_____

2. Are you willing to lay it all at the foot of the cross for Jesus to heal, or are there parts you're holding onto? If so, why?

_____

_____

_____

_____

3. Imagine working at a grocery store and it's time to take inventory. You have new boxes of inventory that must go on the shelf, but first it's important to evaluate where you are today before you place these new items out. (Can't be leaving that expired stuff on the shelves!) What would the shelf look like if you were to take "inventory" of your heart; what would you find regarding good fruit and bad fruit? (As in, what hinders you and what helps you grow.)

_____

_____

_____

_____

4. What does the above passage say about you here? Write down some key words. (Ephesians 4:17–31)

_____

_____

_____

_____

5. In Galatians 5:22–23, it gives you a list of the good fruits given by the Holy Spirit. Write those in the provided space. Do you believe you have these?

_____

_____

_____

_____

Week 2

I had been married to my husband for a very short time when I realized that some of the things I had been carrying as a single person most of my life were things I would have to lay down at the foot of the cross in order to fully become whole with the man God had strategically picked for me. *Dissociative amnesia* is what it's called when your brain blocks out traumatic events, and I had spent most of my life running and filling voids I didn't even know I had as a result of it. I had spent most of my life feeling every bit like an alien in the family that I came from. The traumatic events I could remember haunted me, and even the ones I couldn't recall at the time would eventually surface and come to light, ultimately affecting every piece of my life. The ones surrounding me would suffer at the hand of what had been inflicted on me. Although it was no fault of theirs. Unless I decided to step up to the plate and fight off the generational curses that had trickled down from generations before me.

I don't recall the exact moment it happened or when the memories came back exactly. I just remember knowing that I couldn't hold them in anymore once they did resurface. I felt like a ticking time bomb that was just waiting for the right place to ignite. I wanted to pack them away in a suitcase and leave it somewhere while I ran far, far away from it. I was twenty-five years old when I sat on the front porch watching the sunset fade away, when I told someone for the first time about my sexual abuse and who the first abuser was. I remember sitting in that same place and sobbing for what felt like hours. I felt so disgusted, so unworthy. I felt as if I had been robbed. I had an underlying anger toward God for allowing me to suddenly recall all these things. The memories and the nightmares were like reliving the moments—all over again. And if it were my choice, they could have remained in the dark all while gathering dust. The problem with my way, however, is when we choose to keep things in the dark, Jesus's light can't do what His light is intended to do. It can't drown out the darkness that begins to consume us. It can't heal us.

> Jesus spoke to the people once more and said, "I am the light of the world. If you follow me, you won't have to walk in darkness, because you will have the light that leads to life. (John 8:12 NLT)

I had spent months praying up to this point that God would peel away the layers to get to the heart of who He wanted me to be after my mission trip. Not who I wanted to be, but who He wanted me to be. And although I heard many a time from other believers, "Be careful what you pray for!" I was desperate to find who I was; I was desperate to be anyone but the person I had been. I was praying the prayers that everyone else stirred away from because they were too "dangerous." I hadn't always been the girl that played things safe, anyways. My grandmother always made jokes that had I been the first grandchild, she'd had paid for me to be the last—ha! I was asking for every ounce of me to fall off so I would become less of what the enemy wanted and tried for me to be and more of what God created me to be. Where God is intentional in our creation, the enemy is intentional in destroying it. And I can tell you one thing, it felt as if I had a bull's-eye the size of Africa on my back.

I had realized that I had carried some heavy baggage into my marriage, and at that point, I still had many skeletons hanging in a closet I had no intention of ever opening.

It was in the preparation of my first time giving my testimony that things started to really begin to surface. One of my best friends had asked me to speak to women at a women's tea event at her church, and—with prayer—I agreed. Mistake not, I was nervous leading up to this event but had written out the pieces the Holy Spirit had led me to share. As I began to speak these to my husband—I saw a shift in his facial expression. The environment started to shift, and I could feel the confusion radiating from him. As I wrapped up my "preview" to him, he sat in silence for a moment as I continued to study his body language. He then replied, "That was good, honey." But I knew.

We'd talked about many things before we got married. So I don't want you to read this and leave here with the idea that we never spoke about these things because, I promise, that wasn't the case at all. I just, first off, never knew the extent of some of the trauma, and I, second off, had hoped and prayed this piece of my life would fade away like a sunset in the rearview mirror. It unfortunately did not. And the reason it didn't was because in order to heal from it, I would have to let myself feel and experience exactly what my brain prevented me from doing. Sometimes, whenever we have wounds, we must take the bandage off long enough to allow the wound to heal by exposing it. And at this point in my journey, many of my wounds were seemingly very fresh.

I knew this wasn't the end of the conversation, although I very much hoped it would be. The last thing I ever wanted to do was give the person I trusted with my entirety a reason to not love me. Heck, I wasn't even sure at the time if I could ever come to a place where I loved and valued myself. How could I expect the same from him? The tension became thick, and the words became thin. We were both avoiding the elephant in the room. And I was kind of okay with that.

We were both hurting, we were both confused, and both lost. I wanted him to always see just the best parts of me. But when you become one, it doesn't exactly work that way. Just like God wants every piece of us, our marriages require the same. I had in fact shared my body willingly repeatedly to less than deserving men countless times before my husband because I believed it was the easiest and best thing to love about me (no arrogance here, ladies, I promise), but sharing my soul, sharing the depths of *me*, was a whole other level of vulnerable no one had ever seen from me.

We were on the way to eat for our anniversary, and because there was a lengthy drive involved, this car ride would ultimately become the place where doors opened. I, however, was not prepared for the depth of sorrow that would come with it. I wasn't prepared for the extent of the talking I would have to do to satisfy his wandering mind. My husband's always been one who likes to fix things. He's been that way since I've known him. He needs to understand every little detail, and then he just wants to fix it. And usually, it's one of the things I love most about him. His knowledge and wisdom, his intention to learn everything. But in this moment, I hated that trait with every fiber of my being. He poked and he poked, and he pried, and then he pried some more, and my anxiety began to spiral out of control.

I was completely out of control of this situation, and that angered me. I wanted to keep this all to myself. I wanted it to just go away on its own. Tempers rose, and so did our voices; tears began to slowly fall down my face. As I word-vomited everything I possibly could in a matter of a minute, I screamed "THERE! Are you happy now?"

Thinking back to that moment in the car now, my more "mature" self is cringing. I'm currently saying to myself, *Are you happy? Really, Haley?* Because as if my husband wasn't also hurting in this moment at the fact that I had been hurt and abused repeatedly, and he had no idea of the extent of it until just now. But in that moment, the only thing I could see was my hurt. My focal point was me at that time; a very selfish viewpoint, obviously. I hear so often people say, "Hurt people, hurt people," and although there's much truth in that, the flip side is that broken people reach broken people. My story had a purpose. My brokenness needed to be brought to light so I could heal and so it could help others. Just like yours does. The thing is, whenever we allow God to have the pieces of us that are in shambles, He can put them back together and make a beautiful masterpiece. One in which the enemy can no longer use us as ammunition against us to keep us defeated, oppressed, or depressed.

And although this moment hurt for both of us, it was the door that needed to be opened to begin a complete healing process for me.

We spoke last week in this study about taking inventory of our hearts because everything we do flows from it. The Bible tells us multiple times to guard our hearts, and rightfully so.

It resembles a garden—whenever we choose to leave weeds in it, they'll eventually choke out the good plants that are bearing good fruit. And this is when our identity in Christ shifts into mirroring that of an identity of the world.

I realized that in my brokenness, I wasn't just a broken person with no value; it was in fact, the complete opposite. I held that much more value because of my brokenness. I was a project of God Himself. In my brokenness, Jesus was trying to break down the pieces of me that I was holding onto. All the parts of me that I wasn't confident that He could love, value, or fix; I wanted to keep some of these parts of my life to myself in hopes that I could handle and heal before I went to the foot of the cross. As if He couldn't love me the way I already was. It was kind of my perception of my marriage too. I was fearful that if my sweet husband and even God realized I could not measure up, I would be cut off. That would be it, and I would be alone.

I had spent most of my life trying to earn the love of men because of my childhood. I was trying to fill a void that seemed to never get full. I felt if I had something that was valued enough, I would be wanted in a way that felt good for me. One where I would be the first pick and I would be the chosen one. It wasn't until this moment, in this healing, that I had realized why.

There's no denying that my homelife was much more than what the outside world even knew about. I unfortunately received the blunt force of it as the youngest child. Most of my actions as a young teen were a result of crying out for help. A help that only Jesus could offer and I could and would deny, over and over again.

And I don't say that to stir away from the responsibility of my actions. Hear me out here. Every single day that we are here on this earth, you and I will have to make decisions. We aren't puppets. We are given free will, and our actions will ultimately affect our lives and the ones around us as well. Make no mistake, I made the choices I made, and whether those choices were from a bad heart or a good heart, I made them. My parents, the men, my friend group, my abusers—they are not responsible for my reaction to their actions. Please know in reading that last sentence, it's taken years to even be able to speak those words. It's been a consistent daily task of saying, "I forgive you; you owe me nothing." Because sometimes, even if we don't *feel* they're deserving, sometimes whenever we don't *feel* they are worthy of forgiveness, we must remember, forgiveness is an action and not merely based on our emotions.

By the grace of God, my forgiveness comes from a sovereign forgiver. The ultimate forgiver that forgave me when I needed the same forgiveness as my abusers. It covers me just as much as it covers them. And just as my debt was paid in full the day Jesus went to the cross, so was theirs and so was yours. I don't care what skeletons you have sitting in your closet. Jesus went for you too. Jesus's atonement gives us everlasting forgiveness, and there's not a sin too large for it. There's nothing you can do to change that. There's nothing you can do to cancel out the work on the cross that day.

Bible passage to read:

- John 4:1–42
- Matthew 7:20
- Colossians 3:12–14
- Luke 17:4

Notes:

Where the Word tells you, you are enough; the enemy will tell you, you can't do it—you're not equipped—you don't have what it takes.

Where the Word/Jesus tells you, you are more precious than rubies, the enemy tells you you're ugly, you'll never measure up, you'll never be loved. If we focus on what we aren't, we will never measure up. We will never be enough; we will never have what it takes. We will never be smart enough or pretty enough or capable enough.

Unforgiveness and bad fruit have much in common. Remember, you're the one fueling your plants. You're the one fueling them with either good nutrients (promises) or bad nutrients (lies).

It's important to equip yourselves with the promises of the Lord. Because there's an enemy that's watching you right now. He's waiting to use your greatest "weakness" against you. He's plotting to come after your marriages, your families, your children, your health, your sanity. When is enough, enough? When do you start to fight back with the weapons that have been given to you? It will take work, there's no question about that. But first, we attack the roots in our hearts that pour out into our external lives. Then we discover who we are *in Christ*. If you want things to change, you will have to buckle down and put in the work. Starting today. God doesn't want your watered-down excuses. He wants you; He wants your heart; He wants a relationship with you.

Self-evaluation time

1. Is there something that you're carrying or holding onto internally that is affecting your life externally? Write that below.

_____

_____

_____

_____

2. While reading the story of the woman at the well (John 4:1–42), what stuck out the most to you about this story? And why? (Remember, there's always a reason something becomes "bold" to you on a page in the Bible—take notes when it does. Even if you don't understand the why right now.)

_____

_____

_____

_____

3. How do you see yourself through the eyes of God? If you're having issues with an answer, I want you to write down what God says about you in the Bible. (I am not giving you passages because you need to be able to utilize the word to fight off the

enemy who has you believing you are less than what God has created you to be. It is indeed a Bible study book, my sweet friends!)

_____

_____

_____

_____

4. Read the story of the woman at the well again. Do you see where the Samaritan woman was so desperate to avoid returning to the well that she was willing to entertain this conversation with a Jew for a permanent source? She was desperate; are you? What does verse 13 say about being thirsty? Write it down.

_____

_____

_____

_____

5. Where else in the Bible can you find an instance where God used a woman for His glory? Write it down below and why God chose her.

_____

_____

_____

_____

Week 3

One day, my son and daughter and I were out on our back patio area that was surrounded above by blankets of trees and their branches. And as fall began to slowly creep upon us, those leaves from those branches began to rain in abundance on the patio area. We were still in that weird season where you need a long sleeve on in the morning and then a tank top in the afternoon, so, of course, there were still bees buzzing around. Therefore, we tried to keep the patio clear because both of my kids typically are outside without any shoes on. This day, each one of us had brooms and were working together to sweep the leaves away. My two-year-old son had the broom that had a hard wooden handle on it, while my daughter and I had the plastic ones.

I leaned over to pick something up when my son hit me as hard as he could across the side of my face with that wooden handle. I like to think my pain tolerance is rather high, and maybe that's just what everyone thinks and says. But this is my story, so we are going with it! I kneeled on one of my knees after that good smack to the face, grasping my ear because it hurt the most. My son, on the other hand, had no clue he had even done it. He was literally playing with another toy while I was knelt down suffering. He came over to me not even a minute later, wanting me to pick him up, and in that moment, I was kind of mad at him. It's just an instant reaction, okay? If you're reading this and you're a mom, you know exactly what I am talking about.

There I was, still holding my ear while it pulsated, and he was tugging on my arms to wrap them around him to pick him up.

I had to decide to forgive him rather quickly before he got all bent out of shape at my delay in response to his desire for me to pick him up. Or I could choose to be mad at him for nearly knocking his own mom out and let him just sit there, feeling completely confused and rejected. Obviously, as a mom, I had to forgive him and pick him up. He was innocent; he had no idea what kind of harm he had done with the "weapon" I had given him; all he knew was that he just wanted Mom, and as a parent, my arms were always to remain open to him.

You probably see where I am going here with this, but humor me anyways.

I had a choice to make in that moment, and it would impact me, and it would impact him. And possibly impact him negatively if I chose the wrong response or the wrong decision. Had I made a choice to hold onto the mistake he had made unintentionally, he would have been confused, and I would have remained angry.

I needed to be a mirrored image of God in this moment. He literally sent His son to die on the cross for this type of situation, for this moment, for this very moment of free will of choice. And in that moment of crucifixion, we received the gift given to us known as forgiveness, forever and ever. It was the ultimate sacrifice for you and me. His son had His hands nailed to the cross and our names were on them. Our sins were the thorns that were shoved into His scalp that day. And still, God says, *It's okay, I forgive you, daughter.* And so I forgave my son, and I grabbed him up.

We've talked some in this study about bearing good and bad fruit. We've talked about tending to our gardens and pulling weeds. It takes us back to taking inventory of our lives, digging up the bad roots that have been planted in our hearts over the years and chucking them out so they no longer have a source of nutrients to grow off of. Because quite frankly, whenever we leave them as is—when we try to compress them down so we don't have to face or deal with them—you can find that the person watering those weeds (sometimes unintentionally) that are bearing bad fruit is you.

I'm not sure what those roots with sprouting weeds mean to you. Maybe it's depression, maybe it's anxiety, or sexual abuse, or rejection, or lust, or affairs, or worth, or broken relationships. Whenever we don't deal with these things with the assistance of God doing all the healing rather than ourselves; they will in fact deal with us and flow into every single part of our lives. In more cases than not, the bad things we carry in our hearts, they affect our vision of Christ.

Much of my childhood was complete chaos, and unfortunately, most of the memories I have are not good ones. I was an unplanned pregnancy, and I wasn't exactly something people were cheering for when the news made its way around. My dad even so much as told me that he hung up on my mom the day she called him and told him she was pregnant again. I believe my parents wanted good, and I believe they started there. But because we live in a very corrupt world where the only hope we have is found in God and His Word, they fell into the world rather than the Word. By the time I had gotten to the age of really picking up on things going on within our home, I had already been sexually assaulted multiple times. My vision of family, of love, of everything had been completely construed into some twisted version of "normal."

As things progressively worsened, I found myself being placed with my grandparents several times because of the occurrences within our home. The addiction ran rampant, and everyone seemed to be either in complete denial or completely enabling the pill problem.

My mom was what seemed like a lost soul, and I seemed to be the black sheep of the family. I felt like some stranger in this family I had been born into and could never really make sense of it. Not until I was older, anyways. It was whenever I found that fire within; the one where I wanted people to see themselves like Jesus sees them. The one where you could be the woman at the well and still be loved with depth and meaning. The love that knows who you are, for all your mistakes and sins, and still views you as worthy, enough, and purified. It was in that moment that whenever I fully received that love, that grace, that I could finally see the broken people around me through a lens I was once completely blinded to before. And in that moment, I was finally able to see my own mom as another broken human that Jesus wanted surrender from. It was at that time that I finally got it. She was a child of God, and I couldn't be another stumbling block for her in this life. I had to bridge the gap for her. This was my time to be an example of God's love.

And I had that opportunity weeks before I got married, followed by a lunch with my parents. I was reluctant to even say *yes* to this lunch, but I did anyways. And as we walked to the car, I felt the Holy Spirit pulling me, pulling me to just speak to her. In that moment, I had no clue what words were going to flow from my lips, but whenever I was obedient to the tugging, I felt from the one within me—what needed to be said was said. I can't recall every word, but I can tell you what I do remember. Mainly because I knew it wasn't only a message for her that day; it was one for me as well.

And maybe…just maybe, it's a message for you reading this today.

"Mom, I know you've been carrying the weight of the world most of your life, but God loves you, and He never intended for you to carry those things. He never intended for you to go through life with that heaviness. He just wants you. He forgives you, I forgive you. I know that life hasn't always been peaches and cream for us. But I love you and so does God. I forgive you, Mom."

I knew the words pierced somewhere deep as she sobbed uncontrollably, but I had no idea of the depths of that until a few weeks later, shortly after my wedding day.

It was in the wee hours of the morning when I heard my dad choke back tears as he spoke out the words, "She's gone, Haley. She's gone."

It had been six short days after my wedding day when I had seen her dressed in a gorgeous burgundy and cream dress. It had been six days since she walked over to the table my husband and I sat at and said, "I love you, Haley," and then began to walk out the church doors. She very subtly looked back and smiled at me, and then she was gone. Forever. Six days. My entire life went from being the most perfect example of forgiveness and love to grief and confusion.

That was it. Life changes that quickly.

It was the night of the accident; we'd been at the house all day waiting for police officers and the funeral home to arrive to go over everything. She'd been in a car accident just a few short miles from my parents' home. We were all so exhausted and beaten. But it was that night, that night, my dad finally turned his phone off and drifted off to sleep in the recliner. I was still unable to sleep, and my sister sat on the other end of the couch. It was well past midnight when I heard a *ding* from the side table. I knew it wasn't my dad's because his phone was lying right next to him, and he had turned it off before drifting off, so I just ignored it. And then, again, another *ding*.

Finally, I saw the iPad on the table and picked it up. This thing had been sitting there all day with us and had never made a sound; it was connected to my mom's phone, which was destroyed in the car accident. But here it was, dinging. Once I clicked it to open, I saw what it was. I was completely shaken but in awe too. My mom had downloaded a Bible app and a devotional to remind her every night before she left for work. My mom…she was reading the Bible. She was studying the Word. The best part was the Bible verse on the screen for that night's devotional showed:

> For everything there is a season,
> A time for every activity under heaven.
> A time to be born and a time to die.
> A time to plant and a time to harvest.
> A time to kill and a time to heal.
> A time to tear down and a time to build up.
> A time to cry and a time to laugh.
> A time to grieve and a time to dance.
> A time to scatter stones and a time to gather stones.
> A time to embrace and a time to turn away.
> A time to search and a time to quit searching.
> A time to keep and a time to throw away.
> A time to tear and a time to mend.
> A time to be quite and a time to speak.
> A time to love and a time to hate.
> A time for war and a time for peace.
> (Ecclesiastes 3:1–8 NLT)

There's, quite frankly, a time for everything, and God's timing is always perfect. He has a plan for everyone. There was work moving in my mom that I had no idea about. My mom knew Him. And I believe this verse was one of strategy of comfort, of peace. I just knew at that very moment, I had to be thankful I acted in faith and obedience whenever I was nudged to speak to her, a word directly from the one who would soon be cradling her in His arms. There's something special that in the moment of surrender of Jesus on the cross, His arms were spread wide to bear the nails in the palms of His hands for you and me. The exact same position that He holds His arms open waiting for us to run into them in our moment of surrender. My mom was in God's hands in a way I could ever only have dreamed of. For me, my prayer was that He would save her. And although my prayers weren't answered according to my vision, they were answered in a way I will forever be thankful for. My mom will spend eternity in heaven—one without addiction, one without assault, one without depression or pain or suffering.

Forgiveness is a choice. It's one that holds value not only in our lives but sometimes in the lives of other believers and even nonbelievers. It doesn't mean that the person(s) that did you wrong, the person(s) that hurt you, the person(s) that have rejected, abused, threw you away, said you weren't enough, left you for dead, abandoned you are *off the hook*. This means that you are *no longer* their accuser; you are no longer letting them hold so many pieces of your everyday life. You're choosing to no longer carry the weight of what could have been or what should have been.

> Since God chose you to be the holy people he loves, you must clothe yourselves with tenderhearted mercy, kindness, humility, gentleness, and patience. Make allowance for each other's faults, and forgive anyone who offends you. Remember, the Lord forgave you, so you must forgive others. Above all, clothes yourselves with love, which binds us all together in perfect harmony. And let the peace that comes from Christ rule in your hearts. For as members of one body you are called to live in peace. And always be thankful. (Colossians 3:12–15 NLT)

I want you to look at it as if you're in an airport, and everyone in the airport begins to bring you some of their luggage to hold. You only have two arms, though. One bag after another slowly begins to void your vision as the people begin to stack their bags in your arms. The luggage begins to get heavy, and it's not even yours to carry. You become tired, you become frustrated, and you become anxious because you were not, for a second, intended to be a baggage carousel. Not for yourself and not for other people.

Those bags, the ones weighing you down and stopping you from moving forward, drop them. Let them go. They're not yours to carry anymore. You can't be a replica of a continuous forgiving Father when you can't even forgive other equal sinners. Much less, yourself.

Bible passage to read:

- Luke 17:11–19
- Luke 24:46–49
- Acts 13:38–40
- Hebrews 9:22–24

Notes:

Sometimes you must acknowledge the fact that the world gave you what seems like a losing hand, and there's a Father that can straighten what was dealt out. When you can acknowledge it for what it is, when you can say, "This kind of sucks, God, but I'm here; I am thankful for this season of life. I am thankful for you," the enemy begins to shatter in fear, maybe even a little disbelief. Because in that moment, you've surrendered the very thing that the enemy intended to kill you, destroy you, to scare you, to distract you. You've surrendered it to the only one who can quite literally go before you and fight your battles for you. It's so much easier to have faith when things are going exactly as we envisioned and planned for. But in the moments when our entire life seems to be falling to crumbs around us, our integrity really shows its face. We make forgiveness about us when it's about Jesus. It's about His purpose and our assignment.

Self-evaluation time:

1. Is there someone specific today that you are struggling to forgive
    and let "off the hook" for their sins? Write their name(s) down
    below.

    _____

    _____

    _____

    _____

2. What's holding you back from forgiving them?

    _____

    _____

    _____

    _____

3. What does grace mean to you? Is it free?

    _____

    _____

    _____

    _____

4. I want you to study the Bible for twenty minutes now. No inter-
    ruptions, no phones, just you and Jesus and the Bible. Now, find
    two Bible verses that stick with you. That quite literally meet
    you in your mess, and write those down below. Why are these
    significant to you right now?

    _____

    _____

    _____

    _____

5. Go to Hebrews 12, and read verses 14 through 15. A root of bitterness can flow from unresolved forgiveness when we nurse our hurts and pain. How does this pertain to your life right now?

_____

_____

_____

_____

Week 4

Do you remember what it was like to be spun around? Maybe it was your dad or uncle or grandpa. But whenever they would put you down, it was kind of funny for everyone else that was watching, as you would be stumbling all over the place trying to walk straight. Even sometimes fall.

That's kind of what I envisioned whenever I thought about my life for the last four years. Like maybe someone had been spinning me around, and then I was stuck at the part where you're in the middle of going down for a fall and everything is spinning around you. Except this wasn't exactly fun. It was far from it.

I felt like from the moment I lost my mom, my world slowly began to crumble to pieces around me right where I stood. My soul was exhausted, and I couldn't, for the life of me, shake off the season of life that had quite frankly dragged me through the dirt. There was absolutely nothing superficial about the work needed regarding my integrity, my faith, and my walk. I knew I needed a complete makeover, a complete manifestation of peace to happen internally. There was warfare raging within me between what I wanted and what I needed. Grief had done all but swallowed me whole after my mom was killed in the tragic car accident. My heart was literally aching for the vast majority of this season.

It was shortly after my mom passed, I became pregnant with my second child. And then a few short months later, I lost the woman who practically raised me. The woman whom I swore I was an actual clone of—my grandmother. And then two months later, my papaw. The man who was a clear example of how love speaks loudly. The man who was a believer in hugs and kisses, the one who would have found a way to hang the moon had I asked. He'd always say, "I love you a bushel and a peck and a hug around the neck."

I was still trying to heal from the first spin in my life that left me in shambles on the floor. And then, the punches, they just kept coming. For me, it was like envisioning an open wound and pouring salt directly into it. Not once, but now twice.

In this season of life, more than anything, I really wanted to speed right past the valley I was fixing to take a walk through and speed right up the mountain where the air was lighter and the view was prettier. Because if you knew me, you would know I am a chipper human despite all odds. I grew up with grandparents who worked hard and never knew what the term *lazy* was. They gardened, they hustled, they held down schedules, canned, cooked, and paid the bills. They loved others, they served others. And because of them, my life essentially was a replica of that. I was like an Energizer bunny that just never stopped. I was always going at a high speed with very little ability to slow down and just rest. It's interesting because when you're running a marathon on a flat surface, things are easier. But when you're trying to run at the same pace up a substantially large hill, your endurance becomes compromised. You begin to slow down because your body kind of forces you to as your muscles work actively to get you up the hill. I was running up a hill.

And although my hard-core driven abilities passed as "okay" for most of my life, it was in this season (very long season, might I add) of grief when things began to come to a screeching halt in my life, where I realized that my ability to do all things, carry everyone's burdens, and say *yes* to everything, was me avoiding the very things I needed to heal from. I knew if I could just keep myself busy, if I could just focus on everyone else's hurts and burdens, if I could just keep my mind continuously active on everything else, maybe I wouldn't have to face the things that were haunting me—the things that were affecting me in receiving Christ in a way that I would fully surrender as His chosen daughter, as His purified, beautifully cleaned daughter. I had gotten stuck in grief. Quite literally stuck. The enemy had me bound up in what I believed should have been, in what I wanted and what I desired.

The reality of my high capacity and my high-strung personality was a deflection. And it was shortly after my son turned one when God would allow the enemy to lure me in a season of cracking so I would finally surrender.

From the moment I became a mom, the moment I became a wife, I knew (or felt) I had to keep things in and under my control for things to run smoothly and for me to be able to keep everyone in line. I knew if things were under my control, then I wouldn't be left disappointed, rejected, and let down. Everyone else had to live up to my perfect expectations. This is ultimately a trauma response. And I realized my trauma had to continue to surface so it could be healed and used. Me, being me, I had to be in a complete state of desperation. Just like any other severely hardheaded human being, I had to be at the brink of rock bottom before I would get it.

My son was vaccine-injured shortly after his first birthday, around fifteen months to be exact, and our lives completely changed. Everything came to a screeching halt, and my entire ability to control things evaporated. There was nothing about this season of life I could control or felt I had control of. But I felt out of control because I was never designed to be in control in the first place.

So many times, I would drive home from therapy just weeping after my son had a full-fledged meltdown out of frustration. Ultimately, being hit and scratched and my hair even being pulled and ripped out. He would be so mad because he wanted nothing more than to speak. He wanted people to understand what he wanted, and nobody did. A brilliant, brilliant little boy, and he didn't understand any more than we did. Day after day, night after night of prayer, crying, and just a deep underlying root of anger.

There were so many nights he may not sleep at all. He would just cry, and we had no idea what was wrong with him. I began to worry if something was wrong with him. Is he sick? Does his ears hurt? Maybe it's his stomach? Doctor visit after doctor visit—nothing.

Going to the doctor was a whole other act of war that sent my anxiety through the roof. He was terrified of the doctors' offices after a horrible hospital stay due to an infection. Every blood work and exam, it would take three to four nurses holding him down just to be examined. I was now operating my life out of fear.

I had spent months upon months grieving the actual physical loss of the ones I loved, only to realize that grief wasn't just about burying the people you love in life. But sometimes, it is having to grieve for what you thought should have been. It's grieving what your vision of life should have looked like. And not because God wouldn't be sovereign and not because God wouldn't answer those prayers in his due time, but because in grieving, we must realize that sometimes our vision doesn't line up with God's will. I can't alter God's will for my life. God's will is just that, God's will. Even the enemy can't affect that and must completely surrender to it.

But as someone who needed to be in control, I truly struggled with surrender.

I truly struggled to believe that God could write a happy ending to this story because the only thing I felt I had experienced was hurt after hurt. Disappointment after disappointment. Rejection after rejection. I quite literally waited for the bad news, the loss, the hurt to come knocking on the front door. Heck, I was expecting it, which meant I was constantly waiting for it. It's really hard to see the good when the only thing you're looking for is the bad. I realized in this specific season that it wasn't really about God's ability to heal or answer my prayers, though. It was my inability to view God as my teacher; it was my inability to find comfort in the uncomfortable. It was my unbelief that was the problem, to believe I was worth God giving us a happy ending on this season.

I didn't like being stretched or molded. I didn't like the unknown that came with seasons of what felt like a drought and seasons of valleys. If this was love, it didn't *feel* good. But that's the thing, whenever our emotions are running high, they can make us incompatible with faith. They cloud our judgement of God and the situations we are in because we make it all about us and our feelings. We become problem-focused rather than promise-centered.

And in this specific season, that was me. I was so angry; I was so bitter. I was angry that this could happen to us, that we were having to suffer to this extent. It was quite frankly hard to be transparent in this struggle because I believe there's a misconception as Christians that we should have it all together and put on a happy face in the midst of every struggle. We've made people believe that a "fake it until you make it" mindset is beneficial when it's only actually disregarding the very thing we should be confronting. The constant "well, he's alive and healthy" began to dismiss the actual problem our family was currently enduring with a Band-Aid of "just be thankful." And we were. But it wasn't enough in this season of life because we were hurting, we were grieving. The hurting and the pain only began to fester up because instead of confronting it for what it was, we were just trying to put on happy faces and be thankful. Because that's what you're supposed to do. I was exhausting myself trying to find answers and help. And then one day, it came over me out of nowhere. Surrender, it was about surrender.

As someone who likes to be in control of things, I was trying to control this situation because he was my son. I was trying to heal him and all on my own. I hadn't given him to Jesus; I hadn't given this to Jesus. I was mad because all my attempts were failing, and I was bitter because I was exhausted that everything I was doing wasn't working. All to realize that I do not have the power to heal, God does. I needed and desired God's supernatural healing over my son, and until I was willing to surrender that, I would be stuck in the constant phase of chasing my own tail. I would remain in a season trying to do what God was supposed to do.

This season of life was not an accident.

I had to find a way to find peace in the process.

I was being forced to slow down, to rest, to receive, to surrender.

> Then Jesus said, "come to me, all of you who are weary and carry heavy burdens, and I will give you rest. Take my yoke upon you. Let me teach you, because I am humble and gentle at heart, and you will find rest for your souls. For my yoke is easy to bear and the burden I give you is light." (Matthew 11:28–30 NLT)

Jesus freed me from the burden of trying to be it all in it all. There will be many challenges we face in our lives when we are partnered with Christ.

A *yoke* is defined as a harness made of heavy wood that would go over an oxen's shoulders, which then would be attached to a piece of equipment to pull behind them. I would imagine that whatever it may be they were pulling, it was quite heavy and quite burdensome. The burdens are heavy when we try to carry them ourselves. There's a man on the throne that wants to go before you, that wants to carry the weight of what you're holding on to. He wants to go to war for you, for me. Surrender becomes about making ourselves smaller in the hardships so Jesus can be bigger.

Bible passage to read:

- Luke 7:36–50
- Luke 17:11–19
- Hebrews 11:31–34
- Deuteronomy 31:6

Note:

Whenever I embark on a new health challenge, I typically must force myself to eat healthier and develop healthier habits. Not because I want to, but because I have to. When I fuel my body with healthy things consistently, my body craves those healthy things consistently. But it comes with work, and it comes with discipline. It doesn't mean it's enjoyable, but it is and can be rewarding. The same as the seasons we must walk through in life, the seasons you are being brought to and through are seasons you must endure to understand the value of a healthy relationship with our Lord and Savior. One where you are, in a sense, forced into a season of desperation, where you have to consistently fuel your soul with the promises of the Lord. We learn the value of a Father who provides an everlasting river of thirst-quenching water whenever we are in a season where we feel we are dehydrated, beaten, and exhausted.

Self-evaluation time:

1. What situation in your life today has you believing that God has abandoned you or maybe left you behind?

    _____

    _____

    _____

    _____

2. In Hebrews 11:31–34, you can find that by faith, people overthrew kingdoms and received the things God had promised them. Their moments of weakness were used for strength, and they were strong because of God. What victory do you need to see in your life today? What is it that you need God to give you strength to fight?

    _____

    _____

    _____

    _____

3. What exactly is it that you're unwilling to let go of control over? Maybe it's your schedule or your calendar or sickness or a failed marriage. Write all of them down.

    _____

    _____

    _____

    _____

4. In Luke 17:11–19, what healed the ten men with leprosy?

    _____

    _____

    _____

    _____

5. In Luke 7:36–48, you will find a story about a woman who went to a dinner she wasn't even invited to because she knew

Jesus would be there. She went into a room where she knew she was known, where she knew she was unwelcomed because she was so desperate for her healing through Jesus. And in complete surrender, she fell at His feet and wept while anointing His feet with perfume and her tears. How willing are you to fall at His feet and surrender the very thing that has you stuck in your season of struggle?

_____

_____

_____

_____

6. And last of all, what does Luke 7:36–48 teach you about God?

_____

_____

_____

_____

I n conclusion, I have attached numerous blank pages. I want you to take these pages with you each week after you've done your Bible study, and spend that entire week focusing on the very things we've studied. I want you to journal and write down anything that comes to mind as you begin to self-evaluate and reflect on the things God wants us to work out together. In order to walk our lives full of freedom, we must confront the very things that have kept us bound up and stuck in sinking sand. So make a habit of writing anything down that comes to your mind, because it will over these next four weeks. Be diligent in praying and asking God to reveal the things that have kept you bound up in unforgiveness. Ask God to reveal to you what it is that you need to release from your grip.

Over the last several years in my walk with God, things have been increasingly hard. Not because God doesn't love me but because we do live in a broken world. God has used everything that was intended to harm me to build me. He's healed me in ways I never knew I could receive healing in. He's delivered me from anxiety and depression. He's quite frankly, met me in my mess countless times. He never stops chasing after me because He, in fact, loves and desires me. My heavenly Father is so much bigger than my sin ever was.

That's the very thing that He feels about you, sweet child of the Lord most high.

He values you.

He wants you.

He loves you.

Surrender your version of normal to Him.

Let Him orchestrate all of your days.

My prayer for you:

Father, I pray that the woman holding this book would see herself through a lens that replicates the lens you see her through. I pray that when she sees herself, she sees a clean, free version of herself. That she would be a radiant light that carries you wherever she goes. I pray, Father, that you would remove any type of blinder that prevents her from seeing the very things you want her to see in regard to her own healing. I pray that you would begin to peel back the layers as you help her become the very masterpiece you intended for her to be. I pray for a restored heart as she transitions into a new season of walking out a grace-filled life. That she wouldn't only know what that meant but she could extend that unto others. I pray for her to feel your love overcome her exactly where she is sitting today. I thank you for her. I thank you for your sovereignty, Lord.

Amen.

References

Holy Bible
Tyndale House Foundation. 2015. *Life Application Study Bible*, New
   Living Translation.

Note

About the Author

Haley Kelley grew up in a small town in Western Kentucky. So small, in fact, that it didn't even have a stoplight! Her love for books began at a very young age and stemmed from her grandmother. Haley had the constant desire to write, study, and read. She typically starts her mornings with a cup of coffee, reading her word and her nights are spent studying it. She's a mom to a beautiful daughter and a wild son, and she's married to her best friend, Tyler. They got married in 2017 and moved to a small town in Hopkins County, Kentucky. They have plans and desires to establish a greenhouse on their acreage as well as some farm animals one day! Haley loves to shop, visiting all the hole-in-the-wall restaurants and coffee shops she can find! She found herself leading a women's Bible study when she was brought into the position of creating her own content from the Bible rather than using someone else's content which brought this specific Bible study about. She found much desire in women being able to walk out a life where they could be fully surrendered to God and His purpose for them. Her passion is to help hurting women soar on the backbone of truth in regard to who and whose they are.

Lightning Source UK Ltd.
Milton Keynes UK
UKHW011934280223
417831UK00002B/4